the **WIZARD** of **ID**

SUSPENDED
SENTENCE
INDEED!

Johnny Hart & Brant Parker

FAWCETT GOLD MEDAL • NEW YORK

Library of Congress Catalog Card Number: 84-91029

ISBN 0-499-12645-5

Manufactured in the United States of America

First Ballantine Books Edition: September 1984

10 9 8 7 6 5 4 3 2 1

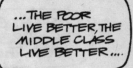

8-3

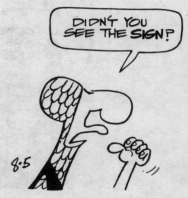

8-5

8-6

8-9

...A MESSAGE FROM THE GOOD REVEREND, SIRE

HE SAID, "THE ROAD TO HELL IS PAVED WITH *GOOD INTENTIONS*"

8-17

...HE ALSO SENT THIS

WHAT IS IT?

A SPEEDING TICKET

RODNEY...THIS BRUTE INSULTED ME!

APOLOGIZE TO THE LADY, OR I DEMAND SATISFACTION!

8·20

UP YOUR NOSTRILS WITH A RUSTY FORK!

I'M SATISFIED IF YOU ARE

8-30

9.2

9-6

BIG PARTY TONIGHT!

I'D LIKE ONE POUND OF HAMBURGER AND SEVEN POUNDS OF CORNMEAL

9-7

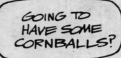

GOING TO HAVE SOME CORNBALLS?

YES, BUT THEY WON'T KNOW THE DIFFERENCE

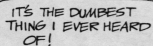

9-15

10-5

10.6

WHERE DO THE JASPERS LIVE?

TAKE KING'S ROAD TO KING'S HIGHWAY.... GO THREE BLOCKS AND TURN LEFT ON KING'S STREET.....

...WHEN YOU COME TO KING'S BOULEVARD TAKE A LEFT...

10-7

YES?

...IT'S THE THIRD HOVEL ON THE LEFT.

10-8

THIS STATUE WILL SERVE AS AN INSPIRATION TO ALL THOSE WHO PURSUE LAW AS A CAREER.

10·9

I THINK IT NEEDS ONE MORE THING...

10.15

10·16

10.22

11-10

ALWAYS FIGHT ON **HIGH GROUND**!

MAKE THE **ENEMY** FIGHT AN UPHILL BATTLE

...IT GIVES YOU A **PSYCHOLOGICAL EDGE**

11-18

PLUS...THEY CAN SEE THE WHITE FLAG FOR **MILES**.

11.23

11·26

...AND ALSO PAST PRESIDENT OF SEVERAL CLUBS AND FRATERNAL ORGANIZATIONS.

12-3

THANK YOU, SIRE.

THE DEPRESSING THING ABOUT BEING SUCCESSFUL IS THAT THEY WRITE YOUR OBITUARY SO FAR IN ADVANCE.

12-8

12-10

I'M SORRY...WE ONLY SERVE MEN IN **THIS** ROOM.

12-11

GOOD... BRING US TWO

12-14

12-18

THERE IT IS, SIRE...THE OFFICIAL KINGDOM TREE...

200 FEET OF MAGNIFICENT EVERGREEN AND IT DIDN'T COST US A CENT!

...IT WAS DONATED BY A LOCAL BUSINESSMAN

I'D LIKE TO SHAKE HIS HAND

12-21

FRED'S HOUSE OF TINSEL AND LIGHTING

GIVE HIM A FULL 180, THEN BRING HIM TO ME.

ROLL
ROLL ROLL ROLL

12·23

IT'S NICE TO TAKE PART IN THE FESTIVITIES.

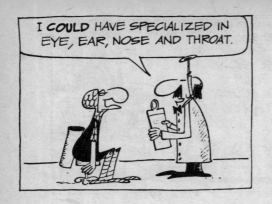

WHAT HAPPENED, BERNIE?

I GOT MUGGED IN THE PARK.

CAN YOU GIVE ME A DESCRIPTION?

1-1

HE'S ABOUT 5'8"....HAS BLACK HAIR AND FOUR TEETH IN HIS KNUCKLES.

1-3

1-6